The Power of Wor

Communication for Everyone

Stephanie

Copyright © [2023]

Title: The Power of Words: Leadership Communication for Everyone
Author's: Stephanie

This book was printed and published by [Publisher's: **Stephanie**] in [2023]

ISBN:

TABLE OF CONTENT

Chapter 7: Leading with Emotional Intelligence

Understanding Emotional Intelligence in Leadership

Communicating Empathy and Understanding

Inspiring and Motivating Others through Emotional Intelligence

Chapter 8: Harnessing the Power of Technology in Communication

Leveraging Social Media for Leadership Communication

Effective Remote Communication Strategies

Ethical Considerations in the Digital Age

Chapter 9: Developing Effective Communication Strategies

Creating a Personalized Communication Plan

Continuously Improving Leadership Communication Skills

Engaging in Lifelong Learning for Effective Communication

Chapter 1: The Importance of Effective Leadership Communication

Understanding the Role of Communication in Leadership

In today's fast-paced and interconnected world, effective communication is an essential skill for successful leadership. Whether you are a CEO, a team leader, or an aspiring entrepreneur, the ability to communicate effectively can make or break your leadership journey. This subchapter aims to explore the pivotal role of communication in leadership and demonstrate how it can benefit individuals from all walks of life.

Communication lies at the heart of leadership, serving as a powerful tool to inspire, motivate, and influence others. A leader's words have the potential to shape minds, build trust, and create a shared vision. By mastering the art of communication, leaders can foster stronger relationships with their teams and stakeholders, leading to increased productivity, collaboration, and ultimately, success.

One of the most significant benefits of effective communication, particularly public speaking, is the ability to inspire and persuade others. Public speaking allows leaders to deliver compelling speeches that resonate with their audience, conveying their vision and goals with clarity and passion. Whether addressing a small team or speaking in front of a large crowd, skilled public speakers have the power to captivate, engage, and motivate others towards a shared purpose.

Moreover, effective communication skills enable leaders to build trust and credibility. By being open, transparent, and empathetic in their interactions, leaders can create an environment of psychological safety, where team members feel comfortable sharing their thoughts, ideas, and concerns. This fosters a culture of collaboration, innovation, and continuous improvement, as individuals feel valued and heard.

Additionally, communication plays a crucial role in conflict resolution and problem-solving. Leaders who can communicate effectively can navigate challenging situations, bridge gaps in understanding, and find win-win solutions. By facilitating open and honest dialogue, leaders can foster an environment where conflicts are addressed constructively, leading to improved teamwork and organizational harmony.

Lastly, communication skills are not limited to traditional leadership roles. The ability to communicate effectively is valuable for individuals in all walks of life. Whether you are a student, a parent, or an employee, mastering communication skills can enhance your personal and professional relationships, boost your confidence, and open doors to new opportunities.

In conclusion, understanding the role of communication in leadership is vital for anyone seeking to make a positive impact in their personal and professional lives. By harnessing the power of words, leaders can inspire, influence, and motivate others to achieve shared goals. Effective communication skills, particularly public speaking, can benefit individuals from all walks of life, fostering trust, collaboration, and success. By recognizing the significance of communication in leadership, we can unlock our full potential and become effective leaders in our respective fields.

The Impact of Words on Leadership Effectiveness

In the realm of leadership, the impact of words cannot be overstated. Words have the power to inspire, motivate, and influence others, making them a crucial tool for effective leadership. Whether in public speaking or everyday communication, the words we choose can shape the perceptions and actions of those around us.

One of the key benefits of public speaking lies in its ability to enhance leadership effectiveness. When leaders take the stage, they have the opportunity to convey their vision, values, and goals to a wide audience. Through carefully crafted words, they can captivate their listeners, instill confidence, and rally support for their ideas.

Public speaking enables leaders to establish a strong presence and command attention. By using compelling language, they can create a lasting impact on their audience, leaving them inspired and motivated to take action. The power of words in public speaking lies in their ability to resonate with individuals on an emotional level, fostering a sense of connection and trust between the leader and their followers.

Moreover, effective communication skills, including public speaking, can enhance a leader's ability to articulate their thoughts and ideas. Clear and concise communication allows leaders to convey their messages in a way that is easily understood, minimizing misunderstandings and promoting a collaborative environment. When leaders are able to express themselves with clarity, they can effectively delegate tasks, provide feedback, and inspire their team members to achieve their full potential.

In addition to public speaking, the impact of words on leadership effectiveness extends to all forms of communication. Leaders must be mindful of the language they use in everyday interactions, as words have the power to shape perceptions and influence behavior. Positive and uplifting words can create a supportive and empowering work environment, fostering a sense of belonging and motivation among team members.

Conversely, negative or careless words can have a detrimental effect on leadership effectiveness. Harsh criticism, blame, or dismissive language can erode trust and create a toxic atmosphere, hindering collaboration and stifling creativity. Leaders must choose their words carefully, ensuring that they align with their values and contribute to a positive and inclusive culture.

In conclusion, the impact of words on leadership effectiveness is undeniable. Public speaking and effective communication skills are essential tools for leaders to inspire, motivate, and influence others. By harnessing the power of words, leaders can create a positive and empowering environment, driving their teams towards success. Whether on the stage or in everyday conversations, leaders must be mindful of the language they use, as it has the potential to shape perceptions, foster trust, and ultimately determine their effectiveness as leaders.

Overcoming Communication Barriers in Leadership

Communication is an essential skill for effective leadership. It is the foundation upon which leaders build relationships, inspire their teams, and influence change. However, communication barriers can hinder the success of a leader, preventing them from achieving their goals and connecting with their audience. In this chapter, we will explore various communication barriers that leaders face and discuss strategies to overcome them.

One of the most common communication barriers is a lack of clarity. Leaders often find themselves overwhelmed with information and ideas, which can result in confusion when trying to convey their message to others. To overcome this barrier, leaders should focus on honing their message, simplifying complex concepts, and using concrete examples to illustrate their points. By providing clear and concise information, leaders can ensure that their message is understood by all.

Another significant barrier is a lack of active listening. Leaders must not only be effective speakers but also attentive listeners. By actively listening to their team members, leaders can gain valuable insights, foster trust, and create a supportive environment. Leaders can overcome this barrier by practicing active listening techniques, such as maintaining eye contact, paraphrasing, and asking open-ended questions. These techniques not only demonstrate respect and empathy but also encourage open and honest communication.

Additionally, cultural and language barriers can pose significant challenges for leaders. In today's globalized world, it is not uncommon for leaders to work with diverse teams from different cultural backgrounds. To overcome these barriers, leaders should strive to understand and appreciate different cultures, customs, and communication styles. They should also ensure that language barriers are addressed by providing translation services or language training when necessary.

Lastly, leaders should be mindful of non-verbal communication barriers. Body language, facial expressions, and tone of voice can convey messages that may contradict or overshadow the spoken words. Leaders should pay attention to their non-verbal cues and ensure that they align with their intended message. By practicing self-awareness and seeking feedback, leaders can overcome these barriers and enhance their overall communication effectiveness.

In conclusion, effective communication is crucial for successful leadership. By addressing and overcoming communication barriers, leaders can connect with their audience, inspire their teams, and achieve their objectives. By focusing on clarity, active listening, cultural understanding, and non-verbal communication, leaders can harness the power of words and become effective communicators in any setting.

Chapter 2: Building Confidence in Public Speaking

Cultivating a Positive Mindset for Public Speaking

Public speaking is a powerful tool that can benefit everyone, regardless of their background or occupation. Whether you are a student, a professional, or a stay-at-home parent, developing strong public speaking skills can have a profound impact on your personal and professional life. However, many individuals are hesitant or anxious about speaking in front of an audience. This subchapter aims to address this fear and provide strategies for cultivating a positive mindset for public speaking.

One of the key benefits of public speaking is the ability to effectively communicate your ideas and thoughts. By honing your public speaking skills, you can articulate your message clearly and concisely, making a lasting impact on your audience. Public speaking also enhances your leadership abilities, as it requires you to command attention and influence others. By becoming a confident and persuasive speaker, you can inspire and motivate others to take action.

However, to reap these benefits, it is crucial to cultivate a positive mindset towards public speaking. The first step is to acknowledge and embrace your fear. Understand that it is natural to feel nervous before speaking in front of an audience, but with practice and preparation, you can overcome this fear. Visualize success and focus on the positive outcomes that public speaking can bring.

Another strategy to cultivate a positive mindset is to practice regularly. The more you practice, the more comfortable and confident you will become. Start by speaking in front of a mirror or a small group of friends and gradually progress to larger audiences. Seeking feedback from trusted individuals can also help you identify areas for improvement and build your confidence.

Furthermore, it is important to adopt a growth mindset when it comes to public speaking. Embrace challenges and view them as opportunities for growth and learning. Understand that even the most accomplished speakers have faced setbacks and made mistakes. By adopting a growth mindset, you can overcome obstacles and continuously improve your public speaking skills.

In conclusion, cultivating a positive mindset is essential for harnessing the benefits of public speaking. By acknowledging and embracing your fear, practicing regularly, and adopting a growth mindset, you can develop into a confident and influential speaker. Public speaking has the power to transform your personal and professional life, opening up countless opportunities for success. So, embrace the power of words and unlock your full potential as a public speaker.

Developing Effective Presentation Skills

Public speaking is a skill that holds immense power. It has the ability to captivate, inspire, and influence an audience. In today's world, where effective communication is crucial, developing presentation skills is more important than ever. Whether you are a student, a professional, or an individual simply looking to enhance your overall communication abilities, mastering the art of public speaking can offer numerous benefits.

One of the key benefits of developing effective presentation skills is the ability to convey your message with clarity and confidence. When you can articulate your thoughts and ideas in a clear and concise manner, you become a more persuasive communicator. This skill can prove invaluable in various areas of life, from delivering a powerful business pitch to expressing your opinions in a social setting.

Furthermore, effective presentation skills can help boost your self-esteem and self-confidence. Many individuals experience anxiety or nervousness when speaking in front of others. However, by honing your presentation skills, you can overcome these obstacles and feel more assured in your abilities. This newfound confidence will not only enhance your public speaking but also positively impact other areas of your life.

Another advantage of developing effective presentation skills is the ability to engage and connect with your audience. A well-delivered presentation has the power to captivate and inspire others. It allows you to establish a connection, build trust, and influence the thoughts and actions of your listeners. Whether you are delivering a speech, leading a team meeting, or even having a one-on-one conversation, the ability to engage and connect with your audience is essential for effective communication.

Additionally, mastering presentation skills can open up numerous professional opportunities. Employers highly value individuals who can effectively communicate their ideas and present them in a compelling manner. By showcasing your presentation skills, you can stand out in job interviews, secure promotions, and excel in your career.

In conclusion, developing effective presentation skills is a valuable endeavor for everyone. The benefits of public speaking are extensive, ranging from enhanced communication abilities to increased self-confidence and improved professional opportunities. By investing time and effort into honing your presentation skills, you can become a more influential and impactful communicator, capable of captivating and inspiring any audience.

Managing Nervousness and Anxiety

Public speaking can be a daunting task for many people. The mere thought of standing in front of a crowd, sharing ideas, and being the center of attention can trigger nervousness and anxiety. However, it is essential to understand that these emotions are entirely normal and can be managed effectively. In this subchapter, we will explore various techniques to help you overcome nervousness and anxiety, allowing you to harness the benefits of public speaking.

1. Preparation is Key: One of the best ways to combat nervousness is through thorough preparation. Take the time to research and organize your thoughts. Practice your speech multiple times, focusing on both content and delivery. The more prepared you are, the more confident you will feel.

2. Deep Breathing and Relaxation Techniques: When anxiety strikes, it is crucial to regain control of your body and mind. Deep breathing exercises, such as inhaling slowly through your nose and exhaling through your mouth, can help calm your nerves. Additionally, practicing relaxation techniques like progressive muscle relaxation can help release tension.

3. Visualize Success: Create a positive mental image of yourself delivering a successful speech. Visualize the audience engaged and responsive. By picturing success, you train your mind to focus on positive outcomes rather than dwelling on potential failures.

4. Embrace Nervous Energy: Instead of trying to suppress nervousness, channel it into enthusiasm. Recognize that some level of nervous energy can enhance your performance by adding passion and

excitement to your delivery. Embrace the adrenaline rush and use it to your advantage.

5. Engage with the Audience: Direct your attention towards the audience rather than fixating on your nerves. Engaging with the audience through eye contact, body language, and interactive questions can help shift your focus away from anxiety and towards the connection you are building with your listeners.

6. Practice Mindfulness: Being present in the moment can help combat nervousness. Focus on the here and now, rather than worrying about what might go wrong. Mindfulness techniques, such as grounding exercises and meditation, can help you stay centered and focused during your speech.

Remember, nervousness is natural and can even be a sign of caring about your message. By implementing these techniques and practicing regularly, you can manage your nervousness and anxiety, allowing you to reap the benefits of public speaking. Embrace the opportunity to share your ideas, connect with others, and become a more effective leader through the power of words.

Chapter 3: Crafting Compelling Messages

Understanding the Power of Words in Leadership Communication

Communication is an essential aspect of effective leadership. The words we choose and how we deliver them can greatly influence our ability to inspire, motivate, and lead others. In this subchapter, we will explore the significance of words in leadership communication and how harnessing their power can benefit everyone.

Words have the power to shape perceptions and create connections. As leaders, the way we communicate can influence how our message is received and interpreted by others. Choosing the right words can help build trust, foster collaboration, and create a positive work environment. Conversely, using the wrong words or miscommunicating can lead to misunderstandings, conflict, and a breakdown in relationships.

Public speaking, in particular, offers numerous benefits for leaders. It provides a platform to share ideas, inspire change, and motivate others towards a common goal. When done effectively, public speaking can captivate an audience, create a sense of unity, and mobilize action. By understanding the power of words in public speaking, leaders can elevate their influence and make a lasting impact on their audience.

One key benefit of mastering public speaking is the ability to inspire and motivate others. Leaders who can effectively communicate their vision and goals can rally their team members and inspire them to give their best effort. A well-delivered speech can ignite passion, boost morale, and foster a sense of purpose among employees. This, in turn, can lead to increased productivity, engagement, and overall team success.

Public speaking also enhances a leader's credibility and presence. When leaders are confident and articulate in their communication, they command respect and authority. This can improve their reputation among colleagues, superiors, and subordinates, leading to greater opportunities for growth and advancement. Additionally, strong communication skills can help leaders navigate difficult conversations, resolve conflicts, and build strong relationships with stakeholders.

In conclusion, understanding the power of words in leadership communication is essential for every leader. By harnessing the power of words, leaders can inspire, motivate, and influence others towards positive change. Public speaking, in particular, offers numerous benefits, including the ability to inspire, enhance credibility, and foster strong relationships. By honing their communication skills, leaders can create a positive work environment, drive team success, and make a lasting impact on their audience.

Creating Clear and Concise Messages

In the realm of leadership communication, one cannot underestimate the power of clear and concise messages. In a world where information overload is the new norm, the ability to effectively convey your thoughts and ideas is a valuable skill that can set you apart as a leader. Whether you are addressing a small team or a large audience, mastering the art of creating clear and concise messages can greatly enhance your communication effectiveness.

Why is clarity and conciseness so important in leadership communication? The benefits are numerous. First and foremost, clear messages ensure that your audience understands your intended message without any confusion or misinterpretation. This is crucial because miscommunication can lead to misunderstandings, conflicts, and even failure to achieve desired outcomes.

Additionally, concise messages are more likely to grab and hold your audience's attention. In today's fast-paced world, people have limited time and attention spans. By delivering your message in a succinct manner, you increase the chances of your audience actually listening and absorbing the information you are conveying.

So, how can you create clear and concise messages? Firstly, it's essential to know your audience. Understanding their needs, preferences, and level of knowledge will enable you to tailor your message accordingly. Avoid using jargon or technical terms that might confuse or alienate your audience. Instead, strive to use simple language that is easy to comprehend.

Another key aspect of creating clear and concise messages is to have a clear structure. Start with a strong opening that grabs attention and clearly states the purpose of your message. Then, organize your ideas logically and present them in a coherent manner. Use bullet points or subheadings to break down complex information into digestible chunks.

Furthermore, remember to be mindful of your tone and delivery. Speak confidently and with conviction, but also be aware of your pacing and clarity of speech. Practice your message beforehand to ensure that you are delivering it in the most effective way possible.

In conclusion, mastering the art of creating clear and concise messages is crucial for effective leadership communication. By ensuring that your message is understood and engaging, you can inspire, motivate, and influence your audience. So, take the time to craft your messages thoughtfully, considering the needs of your audience, and reap the benefits of enhanced communication skills.

Tailoring Messages to Different Audiences

In the realm of effective leadership communication, one crucial skill that often goes overlooked is the ability to tailor messages to different audiences. Understanding the diverse needs, preferences, and expectations of your listeners is a powerful tool that can elevate your communication to new heights. Whether you are addressing a small team, presenting to a board of directors, or speaking in a public forum, this subchapter will provide you with the necessary insights and strategies to engage and connect with any audience.

The benefits of public speaking cannot be overstated. It is a skill that not only allows you to convey your ideas and vision, but also empowers you to inspire, motivate, and influence others. However, to truly harness the power of public speaking, it is essential to recognize that different audiences require different approaches.

One of the key elements in tailoring your message is understanding your audience's background and interests. By conducting thorough research and gathering insights about your listeners, you can craft messages that resonate with their specific needs and aspirations. For example, if you are speaking to a group of professionals in the finance industry, it would be beneficial to incorporate relevant data and industry-specific examples into your speech. On the other hand, if your audience consists of students, using relatable anecdotes and incorporating visual aids can help capture their attention and make your message more memorable.

Another aspect to consider when tailoring messages is the tone and language used. Different audiences respond differently to various communication styles. While a formal and authoritative tone may be appropriate when addressing a board of directors, it might come across as intimidating when speaking to a group of employees. Adapting your language and tone to suit the context and the preferences of your listeners can greatly enhance the effectiveness of your message.

Moreover, understanding the cultural and demographic makeup of your audience is paramount. Recognizing and respecting cultural differences can help you avoid any unintentional misunderstandings or offensive remarks. By being mindful of diverse perspectives, you can ensure that your message is inclusive and relatable to everyone.

In conclusion, tailoring messages to different audiences is a skill that can significantly enhance your leadership communication. By understanding your listeners' backgrounds, adapting your tone and language, and being culturally sensitive, you can captivate any audience and maximize the impact of your messages. Remember, effective communication is not just about what you say, but how you say it.

Chapter 4: Engaging and Persuading Audiences

Captivating Audiences through Storytelling

In today's fast-paced world, effective communication is a crucial skill that can make all the difference in one's personal and professional life. Whether you are a student, a professional, or a homemaker, the ability to captivate audiences through storytelling is an invaluable tool that can elevate your communication skills to new heights. This subchapter titled "Captivating Audiences through Storytelling" from the book "The Power of Words: Leadership Communication for Everyone" aims to unlock the secrets of storytelling and empower you with the ability to engage and inspire any audience.

Storytelling is a timeless art form that has been utilized for centuries to convey messages, share experiences, and connect with others on a deep and emotional level. The benefits of incorporating storytelling into public speaking are immense. By weaving narratives into your speeches or presentations, you can grab the attention of your audience, create an emotional connection, and leave a lasting impact.

One of the key benefits of storytelling in public speaking is that it helps to make complex ideas more relatable and understandable. Instead of bombarding your audience with facts and figures, storytelling allows you to simplify complex concepts by presenting them in a narrative format. This not only helps your audience grasp the information more easily but also enables them to remember it for a longer duration.

Furthermore, storytelling has the power to evoke emotions and create empathy. When you share personal anecdotes or narratives that resonate with your audience's experiences, you establish a common ground, fostering a sense of connection and understanding. This emotional connection makes your message more memorable and encourages your audience to take action.

Moreover, storytelling helps to humanize your message. By sharing personal stories or anecdotes, you become relatable and authentic, enhancing your credibility and trustworthiness. This authenticity not only helps you connect with your audience but also allows them to see you as a genuine and compassionate leader.

In conclusion, captivating audiences through storytelling is a skill that everyone can benefit from. Whether you are a student looking to enhance your presentation skills, a professional aiming to become a persuasive communicator, or someone who simply wants to engage others in meaningful conversations, incorporating storytelling into your public speaking can bring a multitude of benefits. By simplifying complex ideas, evoking emotions, and humanizing your message, storytelling allows you to leave a lasting impact on your audience and become a more effective communicator. So, embrace the power of storytelling and unleash your potential as a captivating speaker.

Utilizing Visual Aids to Enhance Communication

In today's fast-paced world, effective communication is essential for success in all aspects of life. Whether you are a student, a professional, or simply someone who wants to improve their interpersonal skills, the ability to communicate effectively is key. One powerful tool that can greatly enhance communication is the use of visual aids.

Visual aids can take many forms, such as slideshows, charts, diagrams, or even simple props. They serve as powerful tools to support and amplify your message, making it more engaging and memorable for your audience. By incorporating visual aids into your communication, you can achieve several benefits:

1. Increased clarity: Visual aids help clarify complex concepts or ideas that may be difficult to understand through words alone. They provide a visual representation that can simplify information and make it easier for your audience to grasp.

2. Enhanced retention: Studies have shown that people remember information better when it is presented visually. By incorporating visual aids into your communication, you can help your audience retain key points and ideas long after the presentation is over.

3. Improved engagement: Visual aids capture attention and maintain interest. They break up the monotony of a speech or presentation and provide a visually stimulating experience for your audience. This heightened engagement helps to keep your audience focused and interested in what you have to say.

4. Better understanding: Visual aids can bridge language barriers and ensure that your message is understood by a diverse audience. They provide a universal visual language that transcends words, allowing everyone to comprehend your ideas regardless of their native language or cultural background.

5. Increased professionalism: Utilizing visual aids demonstrates your preparedness and professionalism as a speaker. It shows that you have put thought and effort into creating a visually appealing and informative presentation, which can greatly enhance your credibility and authority.

Incorporating visual aids into your communication is not solely limited to formal presentations or public speaking events. They can also be utilized in everyday conversations, meetings, or even personal interactions. By doing so, you can effectively convey your thoughts and ideas, leave a lasting impression, and make your communication more impactful.

Remember, visual aids should complement your verbal message, not replace it. They should be used strategically and sparingly to enhance your communication rather than overwhelm or distract your audience. With practice and attention to detail, you can harness the power of visual aids to become a more effective and influential communicator in every aspect of your life.

Persuasive Techniques for Effective Leadership Communication

In this subchapter, we will explore the art of persuasive techniques in leadership communication. Whether you are a CEO, a manager, or an aspiring leader, mastering persuasive communication is essential for inspiring, motivating, and influencing others. By harnessing the power of words, you can effectively convey your ideas, gain support, and drive positive change within your organization or community.

1. Building Rapport: The first step in persuasive communication is establishing a connection with your audience. Show genuine interest, actively listen, and empathize with their needs and concerns. By building rapport, you create a foundation of trust, making it easier for others to be receptive to your message.

2. Emotional Appeal: People are often motivated by their emotions rather than logic. Use storytelling and vivid language to evoke emotions that resonate with your audience. Appeal to their values, aspirations, and desires, and highlight the positive impact your ideas or initiatives can have on their lives or the organization.

3. Social Proof: Human beings tend to follow the crowd. Use social proof by showcasing success stories, testimonials, or case studies that demonstrate how your ideas or strategies have worked in the past. This helps build credibility and increases the likelihood that others will adopt your viewpoint or support your goals.

4. Credibility and Authority: Establish your expertise and credibility in the subject matter. Share your relevant qualifications, experiences, or achievements to demonstrate that you are knowledgeable and

trustworthy. People are more likely to be persuaded by someone they perceive as credible and authoritative.

5. Clear and Concise Communication: Avoid jargon, complex language, or unnecessary details that may confuse or overwhelm your audience. Clearly articulate your message, ensuring that it is easy to understand and remember. Use simple, concise language to convey your ideas effectively and avoid any ambiguity.

6. Call to Action: To be persuasive, you must provide the audience with a clear call to action. Clearly outline the specific steps or actions you want them to take and explain the benefits they will receive by following your lead. Use strong and compelling language to motivate them to take immediate action.

By employing these persuasive techniques, you can enhance your leadership communication skills and achieve greater success in inspiring and influencing others. Remember, effective leadership communication is not just about speaking, but also about active listening and adapting your message to suit the needs and interests of your audience. With practice, you can become a persuasive communicator who can rally others behind your vision and drive positive change.

Chapter 5: Active Listening and Nonverbal Communication

The Role of Active Listening in Leadership Communication

In the fast-paced and ever-evolving world of leadership communication, one key skill that often gets overlooked is active listening. Effective leaders understand that communication is a two-way street, and that listening is just as important as speaking. In this subchapter, we will explore the crucial role that active listening plays in leadership communication and how it can benefit everyone, regardless of their background or role.

Active listening is the art of fully engaging and understanding what another person is saying, both verbally and non-verbally. It involves giving your undivided attention, asking clarifying questions, and providing feedback to ensure a clear understanding. When leaders actively listen, they create an environment of trust, respect, and open communication, leading to improved relationships, productivity, and overall success.

One of the primary benefits of active listening in leadership communication is that it fosters better understanding and empathy. By truly hearing and comprehending the perspectives, concerns, and ideas of others, leaders can make more informed decisions and develop more effective strategies. Active listening also enhances problem-solving skills, as it allows leaders to identify underlying issues and find creative solutions.

Furthermore, active listening helps leaders build stronger relationships with their team members. When individuals feel heard and valued, they become more engaged and motivated. This leads to higher job satisfaction, increased productivity, and reduced turnover. Additionally, active listening promotes a positive work culture, where everyone's opinions are respected, and collaboration and innovation thrive.

Not only does active listening benefit leaders and their teams, but it also enhances the overall communication climate within an organization. When leaders actively listen, they set an example for others to follow, creating a culture of effective communication. This can lead to improved collaboration, better decision-making, and a stronger sense of shared purpose.

In conclusion, active listening is an essential skill for leaders in all walks of life. By actively listening, leaders can gain a deeper understanding of their team members, build stronger relationships, and create a positive communication climate. Whether you are a manager, entrepreneur, or aspiring leader, mastering active listening will undoubtedly enhance your leadership communication skills and contribute to your success.

Enhancing Nonverbal Communication Skills

Nonverbal communication is a powerful tool that can greatly enhance your public speaking skills. In fact, research suggests that up to 93% of communication is nonverbal, meaning that how you say something can have a far greater impact than the actual words you use. Therefore, mastering nonverbal communication is essential for anyone looking to improve their public speaking abilities.

One key aspect of nonverbal communication is body language. Your posture, gestures, and facial expressions can convey a wealth of information to your audience. By maintaining an open and upright posture, you can exude confidence and engage your listeners. Similarly, using appropriate hand gestures can help emphasize your points and make them more memorable. Facial expressions, such as smiling or maintaining eye contact, can create a connection with your audience and make them feel more engaged.

Another important aspect of nonverbal communication is vocal tone and delivery. The way you speak, including your tone, pitch, and pace, can greatly impact how your message is received. By varying your vocal tone and using pauses effectively, you can add emphasis to certain points and keep your audience engaged. Additionally, speaking with clarity and confidence can help establish your credibility and make your message more persuasive.

Nonverbal communication also extends to your appearance and attire. Dressing appropriately for the occasion can help you make a positive first impression and establish your credibility. Your appearance should reflect your professionalism and the message you want to convey.

Paying attention to grooming and ensuring that your attire is neat and appropriate for the audience can help you command respect and attention.

By enhancing your nonverbal communication skills, you can effectively convey your message and connect with your audience on a deeper level. It allows you to express emotions, engage your listeners, and establish authority. Whether you are delivering a keynote speech, participating in a team meeting, or even having a casual conversation, nonverbal communication plays a crucial role in how your message is perceived.

In conclusion, mastering nonverbal communication skills is vital for anyone looking to improve their public speaking abilities. By paying attention to body language, vocal tone, and appearance, you can enhance your ability to engage and connect with your audience. Remember, the power of words extends beyond what is spoken – it lies in how it is delivered.

Building Trust through Effective Listening

In the fast-paced world we live in, effective communication has become more important than ever. It is not just about speaking confidently or articulating our thoughts clearly; it is also about truly listening to others. In this subchapter, we will explore the concept of building trust through effective listening and how it can benefit everyone, regardless of their background or profession.

Listening is an essential skill that can have a profound impact on our personal and professional relationships. When we truly listen to others, we demonstrate respect, empathy, and understanding. This builds trust and creates a safe space for open and honest communication. By actively listening, we show that we value the opinions and perspectives of others, fostering a sense of belonging and collaboration.

In leadership roles, effective listening is even more critical. When leaders listen attentively to their team members, they promote a culture of trust and transparency. Employees feel valued and heard, which boosts their engagement and productivity. Leaders who prioritize effective listening also gain a deeper understanding of their team's needs, challenges, and aspirations. This knowledge enables them to make informed decisions and provide meaningful support.

Moreover, effective listening is not limited to verbal communication. It extends to nonverbal cues, such as body language and facial expressions. By paying attention to these cues, we can better understand the underlying emotions and thoughts of the person speaking. This helps us respond appropriately and with empathy, strengthening the connection and trust between individuals.

In addition to enhancing relationships, effective listening also improves our problem-solving abilities. By actively listening to different perspectives and ideas, we can gain new insights and find innovative solutions. This is especially beneficial in the workplace, where diverse teams can leverage their collective knowledge and experiences to overcome challenges and drive progress.

In conclusion, building trust through effective listening is a crucial skill for everyone, regardless of their background or profession. By actively listening, we create an environment of trust, respect, and collaboration. This leads to stronger personal and professional relationships, as well as enhanced problem-solving abilities. Therefore, we should all strive to become better listeners and harness the power of effective communication in our daily lives.

Chapter 6: Managing Difficult Conversations

Strategies for Constructive Feedback and Criticism

Providing constructive feedback and criticism is an essential skill for effective communication and growth. In the realm of leadership and public speaking, it becomes even more crucial to master these strategies. Constructive feedback not only helps individuals improve their communication skills but also enhances their overall leadership abilities. In this subchapter, we explore some valuable strategies for delivering feedback and criticism in a constructive manner.

1. Focus on the behavior, not the person: When providing feedback, it is important to separate the behavior from the individual. Instead of making personal attacks, address specific actions or behaviors that can be improved upon. This approach ensures that the feedback is received positively and encourages growth rather than causing defensiveness or resentment.

2. Be specific and objective: Vague feedback is not helpful for the recipient. Instead, provide specific examples and focus on objective observations. Clearly explain what worked well and what areas need improvement, allowing the individual to understand the feedback and take appropriate action.

3. Use the sandwich method: The sandwich method is an effective way to deliver feedback without causing discouragement. Start with a positive comment or commendation, followed by the areas that need improvement, and end with another positive note. This approach

helps maintain a balance between constructive criticism and motivation.

4. Encourage self-reflection: Instead of simply telling someone what they did wrong, encourage them to reflect on their own performance. Ask open-ended questions that help them assess their strengths and weaknesses. This approach promotes self-awareness and empowers individuals to take ownership of their growth.

5. Offer solutions and support: Providing feedback without offering solutions can leave the recipient feeling lost. Along with pointing out areas for improvement, suggest strategies or resources that can help them overcome challenges. Offer your support and let them know you are available for guidance and assistance.

6. Foster a culture of feedback: Cultivating a culture where constructive feedback is welcomed and valued is essential for growth and improvement. Encourage open communication among team members and provide opportunities for them to practice giving and receiving feedback. This allows everyone to learn from one another and continuously improve their communication skills.

By implementing these strategies, you can ensure that your feedback and criticism are constructive and beneficial to all parties involved. Remember, effective feedback helps individuals develop their public speaking skills, enhances leadership abilities, and fosters a positive and growth-oriented environment.

Resolving Conflict through Effective Communication

Conflict is an inevitable part of life. Whether it is in our personal relationships, professional settings, or even within ourselves, conflict can arise and cause stress and tension. However, what sets successful individuals apart is their ability to resolve conflicts through effective communication. In this subchapter, we will explore the power of words in resolving conflicts and how effective communication can benefit us all.

Conflict resolution through effective communication begins with active listening. When we truly listen to others, we are able to understand their perspective, needs, and concerns. By giving our full attention and engaging in active listening, we can avoid misunderstandings and find common ground. This approach fosters empathy and creates a space for open and honest dialogue.

Another crucial aspect of resolving conflicts is choosing our words wisely. Words have immense power and can either escalate or diffuse a conflict. By using respectful and non-confrontational language, we can express our thoughts and emotions without further aggravating the situation. Additionally, choosing the right words allows us to address the core issues at hand, leading to more effective problem-solving.

Furthermore, effective communication involves being assertive while still remaining respectful. It is essential to express our needs, concerns, and boundaries clearly and confidently. However, it is equally important to consider the feelings and perspectives of others. By striking a balance between assertiveness and empathy, we create an environment where all parties feel heard and respected.

Resolving conflict through effective communication also requires the skill of managing emotions. Emotions can often run high during conflicts, and if not handled properly, they can hinder the progress towards resolution. By practicing emotional intelligence and being aware of our own emotions, as well as those of others, we can navigate conflicts with greater ease and reach mutually beneficial outcomes.

The benefits of mastering effective communication for conflict resolution are vast. It strengthens relationships, fosters trust, and promotes a positive work environment. It allows us to address conflicts promptly, preventing them from escalating into larger issues. Additionally, effective communication enhances our problem-solving skills and increases our overall emotional intelligence.

In conclusion, resolving conflicts through effective communication is an essential skill for everyone. By actively listening, choosing our words wisely, being assertive yet respectful, and managing emotions, we can overcome conflicts and build stronger connections with others. The power of words in conflict resolution cannot be underestimated, and by harnessing this power, we can navigate through conflicts with grace, empathy, and understanding.

Navigating Challenging Situations with Diplomacy and Tact

In our daily lives, we often encounter challenging situations that require us to communicate with diplomacy and tact. Whether it's dealing with a difficult colleague, resolving conflicts within a team, or addressing sensitive topics, the way we approach these situations can have a significant impact on the outcome. In this subchapter, we will explore the power of words in navigating such challenges and the benefits of public speaking in developing the necessary skills.

Diplomacy and tact are essential qualities for effective leadership communication. They enable us to convey our message in a respectful and empathetic manner, fostering understanding and cooperation even in the most difficult circumstances. By using the right words, tone, and body language, we can defuse tension, build trust, and find common ground.

One of the key benefits of public speaking is that it equips us with the tools to navigate challenging situations with diplomacy and tact. Through public speaking, we learn to communicate with clarity, confidence, and sensitivity. We develop the ability to choose our words carefully, considering the impact they may have on others. Public speaking also teaches us to listen actively and respond thoughtfully, allowing us to address concerns and objections effectively.

When faced with a challenging situation, it is crucial to remain calm and composed. Take a moment to collect your thoughts and choose your words wisely. Avoid using confrontational or inflammatory language that may escalate the tension. Instead, focus on finding common ground and exploring solutions together. By demonstrating empathy and understanding, you can build bridges, foster positive relationships, and achieve mutually beneficial outcomes.

Another important aspect of navigating challenging situations is active listening. Pay attention to both verbal and non-verbal cues, and seek to understand the underlying motivations and concerns of the other party. By showing genuine interest and empathy, you can create an environment where open and honest dialogue can take place.

In conclusion, mastering the art of navigating challenging situations with diplomacy and tact is crucial for effective leadership communication. The benefits of public speaking in developing these skills cannot be overstated. By harnessing the power of words and employing active listening, we can diffuse tension, build trust, and find mutually beneficial solutions. Whether in personal or professional settings, these skills are invaluable for everyone seeking to excel in their communication abilities and lead with influence.

Chapter 7: Leading with Emotional Intelligence

Understanding Emotional Intelligence in Leadership

Emotional intelligence, often referred to as EQ, is a crucial skill for effective leadership. In the book "The Power of Words: Leadership Communication for Everyone," we explore the concept of emotional intelligence and its significance in the realm of leadership. This subchapter aims to provide a comprehensive understanding of emotional intelligence and how it can be applied to enhance leadership skills.

Leadership is not solely about making decisions, but also about inspiring and motivating others. Emotional intelligence plays a vital role in achieving this. It involves the ability to recognize, understand, and manage both one's own emotions and the emotions of others. By cultivating emotional intelligence, leaders can create a positive and supportive environment, leading to increased productivity and employee satisfaction.

One aspect of emotional intelligence is self-awareness. Leaders who are self-aware understand their own emotions, strengths, weaknesses, and values. This self-awareness allows them to effectively manage their emotions and make decisions that align with their values. Additionally, self-aware leaders can identify their triggers and anticipate how their emotions may impact their decision-making abilities.

Another crucial element of emotional intelligence is empathy. Leaders who are empathetic can understand and share the feelings of others.

This skill enables them to connect with their team members on a deeper level, fostering trust and collaboration. Empathetic leaders can also anticipate the needs and concerns of their employees, leading to improved communication and problem-solving.

Furthermore, emotional intelligence involves effective communication skills. Leaders must be able to express their thoughts and ideas clearly, while also actively listening to others. By effectively communicating, leaders can promote understanding and build strong relationships with their team members.

In the context of leadership, emotional intelligence offers numerous benefits. It enhances self-awareness, allowing leaders to better understand their strengths and weaknesses. It also improves decision-making abilities by enabling leaders to consider the emotional impact of their choices. Emotional intelligence also helps leaders manage conflicts and build stronger relationships, leading to a more harmonious work environment.

Regardless of your background or profession, understanding emotional intelligence is crucial for everyone. Whether you are a CEO, a team leader, or an aspiring entrepreneur, developing emotional intelligence will undoubtedly contribute to your success in leadership.

In conclusion, emotional intelligence is a fundamental aspect of effective leadership. By understanding and applying emotional intelligence, leaders can create a positive work environment, inspire their teams, and achieve remarkable results. In "The Power of Words: Leadership Communication for Everyone," we delve deeper into the topic of emotional intelligence and provide practical strategies for enhancing this essential skill.

Communicating Empathy and Understanding

In today's fast-paced world, effective communication has become more important than ever. It is not just about conveying information, but also about connecting with others on a deeper level. In this subchapter, we will explore the power of empathy and understanding in communication and how it can benefit everyone, regardless of their background or profession.

Empathy is the ability to understand and share the feelings of another person. When we communicate with empathy, we acknowledge and validate the emotions of others. This can be particularly beneficial in public speaking, where the speaker has the opportunity to address a large audience. By showing empathy, speakers can create a sense of connection and establish trust with their listeners.

One of the key benefits of communicating with empathy is that it fosters understanding. When we truly listen to others and try to understand their perspectives, we break down barriers and build bridges of empathy. This is especially important in a diverse society where people come from different cultural, social, and economic backgrounds. By communicating with empathy, we can bridge those gaps and create a more inclusive and harmonious community.

Furthermore, empathy in communication has the power to inspire and motivate others. When we genuinely care about the experiences and challenges of our audience, we can tailor our message to resonate with them. By understanding their needs and concerns, we can provide solutions and offer support. This can be particularly impactful in leadership communication, where inspiring and motivating others is crucial for success.

In addition to empathy, understanding is another essential element in effective communication. When we seek to understand others, we open ourselves up to different perspectives and ideas. This not only enriches our own knowledge but also allows us to communicate more effectively. Understanding enables us to communicate in a way that is relatable and relevant to our audience, ensuring that our message is received and understood.

In conclusion, communicating with empathy and understanding is essential for effective public speaking and communication in general. By showing empathy, we can connect with our audience on a deeper level, fostering understanding and creating a sense of unity. Additionally, understanding allows us to tailor our message to the needs and concerns of our audience, inspiring and motivating them to take action. Whether you are a leader, a student, or anyone interested in improving their communication skills, embracing empathy and understanding will undoubtedly bring you closer to achieving your goals.

Inspiring and Motivating Others through Emotional Intelligence

Emotional intelligence is a key ingredient in the recipe for effective leadership communication. In this subchapter, we will explore how emotional intelligence can be harnessed to inspire and motivate others. Whether you are a seasoned public speaker or someone who shies away from public speaking, understanding the power of emotional intelligence can transform your communication skills and make you an influential leader.

When it comes to inspiring and motivating others, emotional intelligence allows you to connect with your audience on a deeper level. By understanding and managing your own emotions, you can create an environment that fosters trust and empathy. This, in turn, encourages your audience to open up and engage with your message.

As you develop your emotional intelligence, you will become more adept at recognizing and understanding the emotions of others. This enables you to tailor your communication to resonate with their needs and desires. By speaking directly to their emotions, you can inspire and motivate them to take action.

One of the key aspects of emotional intelligence is empathy. By putting yourself in the shoes of your audience, you can truly understand their experiences, challenges, and aspirations. This empathy allows you to craft messages that speak directly to their hearts, connecting with them on a personal level. By appealing to their emotions, you can ignite their passion and drive, encouraging them to embrace new ideas and take bold actions.

In addition to empathy, emotional intelligence also encompasses self-awareness and self-regulation. By being aware of your own emotions and how they affect your communication, you can adapt your approach to match the needs of your audience. This self-awareness also allows you to manage any negative emotions that may hinder your ability to inspire and motivate others.

In summary, emotional intelligence is a powerful tool for inspiring and motivating others. By understanding and managing your own emotions, and by empathizing with your audience, you can create a connection that transcends words. This connection enables you to truly inspire and motivate others to reach their highest potential. So, embrace the power of emotional intelligence and become a leader who can inspire and motivate not just through words, but through the power of emotions.

Chapter 8: Harnessing the Power of Technology in Communication

Leveraging Social Media for Leadership Communication

In today's digital age, social media has become an integral part of our lives. It has revolutionized the way we communicate, connect, and share information. As a leader, it is crucial to recognize the power of social media in enhancing your communication skills and reaching a wider audience. This subchapter aims to explore the benefits of leveraging social media for leadership communication and how it can help you become a more effective and influential leader.

One of the key benefits of using social media for leadership communication is the ability to connect with a diverse audience. Social media platforms such as Facebook, Twitter, LinkedIn, and Instagram allow you to reach individuals from various backgrounds, cultures, and demographics. This enables you to expand your network, engage with a broader range of people, and gain valuable insights and perspectives.

Additionally, social media provides a platform for you to share your ideas, thoughts, and expertise. By consistently posting relevant and insightful content, you position yourself as a thought leader in your industry. This not only enhances your credibility but also increases your visibility and influence within your organization and industry.

Another advantage of leveraging social media for leadership communication is the opportunity to engage in real-time conversations and receive instant feedback. Social media platforms enable you to have direct interactions with your audience, allowing you to address their concerns, answer their questions, and respond to their feedback promptly. This level of engagement fosters a sense of trust and transparency, strengthening your relationship with your followers.

Furthermore, social media allows you to showcase your authentic leadership style. By sharing personal stories, experiences, and behind-the-scenes glimpses, you humanize your leadership and connect with your audience on a deeper level. This authenticity builds trust and loyalty, inspiring others to follow your lead.

However, it is important to note that leveraging social media for leadership communication requires careful planning and strategy. It is crucial to maintain a consistent brand image, ensure your content aligns with your leadership values, and be mindful of your online interactions. Additionally, it is essential to stay updated with the latest social media trends and platforms to effectively engage with your audience.

In conclusion, social media has transformed the way leaders communicate and connect with their audience. By leveraging social media for leadership communication, you can expand your network, position yourself as a thought leader, engage in real-time conversations, showcase your authentic leadership style, and build trust and loyalty. However, it is essential to approach social media communication with careful planning and strategy to maximize its benefits and avoid potential pitfalls. Embrace the power of social media, and elevate your leadership communication to new heights.

Effective Remote Communication Strategies

In today's digital age, remote communication has become an integral part of our personal and professional lives. Whether you are working from home, attending online meetings, or simply connecting with friends and family, the ability to effectively communicate remotely is crucial. This subchapter explores various strategies for mastering remote communication, enabling you to excel in this new era of connectivity.

First and foremost, it is essential to establish clear and concise communication channels. With the availability of numerous communication platforms, such as email, video conferencing, and instant messaging, it is important to choose the right tool for the right purpose. Consider the nature of your message and the level of urgency before deciding on the most appropriate platform. This will ensure that your communication is effective and efficient.

Secondly, effective remote communication requires active listening. When engaging in virtual conversations or meetings, it is crucial to pay close attention to the speaker, taking note of both verbal and non-verbal cues. Active listening helps you understand the speaker's message more accurately, allowing you to respond appropriately and build stronger connections with others.

Another strategy for effective remote communication is to be mindful of your tone and language. Without the benefit of face-to-face interaction, it is easy for messages to be misinterpreted. To avoid misunderstandings, choose your words carefully and consider the tone in which they are delivered. Be respectful, empathetic, and positive in your communication to foster healthy relationships and productive collaborations.

Furthermore, effective remote communication involves utilizing visual aids and technology to enhance your message. When presenting information remotely, make use of slides, videos, and other visual aids to engage your audience and reinforce key points. Additionally, familiarize yourself with the various features of the communication platforms you use, such as screen sharing and virtual whiteboards, to create interactive and dynamic presentations.

Lastly, remember to prioritize building relationships and fostering connections when communicating remotely. Take the time to engage in informal conversations, ask about people's well-being, and show genuine interest in their lives. These small gestures can go a long way in building trust and rapport, even in a remote setting.

In conclusion, mastering effective remote communication is vital in today's interconnected world. By establishing clear communication channels, actively listening, being mindful of tone and language, utilizing visual aids, and prioritizing relationship-building, you can excel in remote communication. These strategies will not only enhance your personal and professional interactions but also contribute to your overall success in the digital age.

Ethical Considerations in the Digital Age

In today's digital age, where information is readily available at our fingertips, it is imperative to address the ethical considerations that arise in the realm of communication. As technology continues to advance, we must navigate the ethical challenges that come with it. This subchapter of "The Power of Words: Leadership Communication for Everyone" delves into the ethical considerations in the digital age and how they impact our daily lives.

The benefits of public speaking are undeniable, empowering individuals to express their thoughts, influence others, and create positive change. However, the rise of digital platforms and social media has opened up a whole new avenue for communication, creating a need for ethical guidelines to ensure responsible and constructive dialogue.

One of the primary ethical considerations in the digital age is the issue of privacy. With the vast amount of personal information available online, it is crucial to respect individuals' privacy rights. This includes obtaining consent before sharing someone's personal information, respecting the boundaries of online communities, and refraining from engaging in cyberbullying or harassment.

Another ethical consideration is the spread of misinformation. With the ease of sharing information online, it is essential to verify the accuracy of the content we share. Misinformation can have severe consequences, such as damaging reputations, spreading fear, or influencing public opinion. Therefore, it is our responsibility to fact-check and ensure the information we disseminate is accurate and reliable.

Additionally, digital communication brings about challenges related to digital citizenship. We must strive to promote respectful and inclusive online environments, where diversity of opinions is welcomed, and hate speech is condemned. Cyberbullying, trolling, and online harassment have become prevalent issues that need to be addressed to maintain a healthy digital ecosystem.

Furthermore, the ethical use of data is a crucial consideration. As we navigate the digital landscape, we must be mindful of the data we generate and share. Companies must handle personal data responsibly, ensuring transparency, consent, and security. Individuals should also be cautious about the information they provide, understanding how it may be used and protected.

In conclusion, ethical considerations in the digital age are essential for maintaining a responsible and constructive communication landscape. Respecting privacy, verifying information, promoting digital citizenship, and safeguarding personal data are all crucial aspects of ethical communication. By understanding and adhering to these ethical guidelines, we can harness the benefits of public speaking and digital communication to create a positive and inclusive digital society for all.

Chapter 9: Developing Effective Communication Strategies

Creating a Personalized Communication Plan

In today's fast-paced world, effective communication skills have become more crucial than ever. Whether you are a business professional, a student, or someone looking to make a positive impact in your personal relationships, developing a personalized communication plan can be a game-changer. This subchapter will guide you through the process of creating a communication plan that suits your unique needs and goals, helping you unlock the power of words and become a more effective communicator.

The benefits of public speaking cannot be overstated. Public speaking skills not only enhance your ability to express yourself clearly and confidently, but they also open up numerous opportunities for personal and professional growth. Whether you want to advance your career, build stronger connections with others, or become a more influential leader, public speaking can help you achieve these goals and more.

To create a personalized communication plan, start by identifying your objectives. What do you hope to achieve through enhanced communication skills? Are you looking to become a better presenter, negotiate more effectively, or simply improve your interpersonal relationships? Once you have a clear understanding of your objectives, you can tailor your plan to meet these specific goals.

Next, assess your strengths and weaknesses as a communicator. Are there particular areas where you excel, such as storytelling or active listening? Conversely, are there areas where you struggle, such as managing conflict or delivering presentations? By identifying your strengths and weaknesses, you can focus your efforts on improving areas that need development while leveraging your existing communication skills.

Consider incorporating various communication techniques and tools into your plan. These may include public speaking workshops, interpersonal communication courses, or even joining a local Toastmasters club. Additionally, you can utilize online resources, such as TED Talks or communication podcasts, to expand your knowledge and gain insights from experts in the field.

Finally, practice, practice, practice! Communication skills are like any other skill – they require consistent practice to improve. Incorporate regular opportunities to practice your newfound skills, whether it's through role-playing exercises, delivering speeches to a small group, or engaging in meaningful conversations with friends and colleagues.

By creating a personalized communication plan, you are taking a proactive step towards becoming a more effective communicator. Remember, effective communication is not just about speaking; it's about connecting with others, fostering understanding, and creating positive change. Embrace the power of words, and watch as your personal and professional life flourishes.

Continuously Improving Leadership Communication Skills

Effective communication is the cornerstone of strong leadership. Whether you are a CEO, manager, or simply looking to enhance your communication abilities, continuously improving your leadership communication skills is essential for success. In this subchapter, we will explore the benefits of public speaking and how it can contribute to your growth as a leader.

Public speaking is a powerful tool that allows leaders to engage and influence their audience. By honing your public speaking skills, you can effectively convey your message, inspire others, and build trust and credibility. One of the key benefits of public speaking is the ability to articulate your ideas with clarity and conviction. As a leader, being able to clearly express your thoughts and vision is crucial in gaining the support and buy-in of your team.

Another benefit of public speaking is the opportunity it provides for personal growth. Stepping out of your comfort zone and addressing a large audience can be intimidating, but it also pushes you to develop skills such as confidence, poise, and effective body language. These qualities not only enhance your public speaking abilities but also translate into improved leadership skills in various situations, such as team meetings, negotiations, and presentations.

Public speaking also allows leaders to foster connections and build relationships. When you speak in front of an audience, you have the chance to connect with individuals from diverse backgrounds and perspectives. By sharing your ideas and experiences, you can initiate meaningful conversations and establish yourself as a thought leader in your industry. This networking opportunity can open doors to collaborations, partnerships, and mentorship, further expanding your influence as a leader.

Moreover, public speaking provides a platform to inspire and motivate others. As a leader, your words have the power to ignite passion and drive in your team members. By delivering engaging and impactful speeches, you can inspire others to embrace change, overcome challenges, and strive for excellence. Public speaking enables you to share your knowledge, experiences, and lessons learned, creating a ripple effect of positive change within your organization and beyond.

In conclusion, continuously improving your leadership communication skills, specifically in public speaking, can bring numerous benefits to your professional growth. From enhancing your ability to articulate ideas to fostering connections and inspiring others, public speaking plays a pivotal role in your journey towards becoming a more effective and influential leader. Embrace the power of words, and unlock your full leadership potential.

Engaging in Lifelong Learning for Effective Communication

In today's fast-paced and ever-changing world, effective communication is a skill that is highly valued and sought after by people from all walks of life. Whether you are a student, a professional, a parent, or simply an individual striving for personal growth, the ability to effectively communicate your thoughts and ideas is crucial for success. One way to enhance this skill is by engaging in lifelong learning, particularly in the realm of public speaking.

Public speaking, often feared by many, has numerous benefits that extend beyond just delivering a speech to a large audience. It is a powerful tool that can transform your personal and professional life. By honing your public speaking skills, you can develop the ability to express yourself confidently, articulate your ideas clearly, and captivate the attention of any audience.

One of the key benefits of public speaking is the boost it gives to your self-confidence. As you continue to engage in public speaking and expand your knowledge in this area, you will gradually overcome the fear of speaking in front of others. This newfound confidence will permeate into other aspects of your life, empowering you to communicate more effectively in all situations, whether it is during a meeting at work, a conversation with a client, or even a casual interaction with friends and family.

Additionally, public speaking allows you to refine your critical thinking and organizational skills. Before stepping onto the stage, you must carefully structure your thoughts, craft a compelling message, and anticipate potential questions or objections. This process enhances your ability to think critically, analyze information, and present a coherent argument. These skills are transferable to various areas of life, enabling you to communicate your ideas with clarity and persuasiveness.

Engaging in lifelong learning for effective communication through public speaking also opens doors to new opportunities. As you become a more skilled speaker, you may find yourself being invited to speak at conferences, seminars, or workshops. These platforms provide an opportunity to share your expertise, expand your network, and establish yourself as a thought leader in your field. Moreover, the ability to communicate effectively can enhance your professional reputation, leading to career advancements and increased opportunities for growth.

In conclusion, the benefits of public speaking are vast and extend beyond the mere act of delivering a speech. Engaging in lifelong learning in this area can boost your self-confidence, refine your critical thinking and organizational skills, and open doors to exciting opportunities. No matter who you are or what your niche is, developing your public speaking skills will undoubtedly enhance your ability to communicate effectively and make a lasting impact on those around you. So, embrace the power of words and embark on a journey of lifelong learning for effective communication.

Chapter 10: Impacts and Outcomes of Effective Leadership Communication

Driving Positive Organizational Culture through Communication

In today's fast-paced world, effective communication is key to success in any organization. Whether you are a leader, manager, or employee, the way you communicate has a significant impact on the overall organizational culture. In this subchapter, we will explore how communication can drive positive organizational culture and why it is crucial for everyone to develop their communication skills.

Communication is the lifeblood of any organization. It connects individuals, teams, and departments, ensuring that everyone is on the same page and working towards common goals. When communication is open, transparent, and constructive, it fosters trust, collaboration, and innovation. On the other hand, poor communication can lead to misunderstandings, conflict, and a toxic work environment.

One of the key ways to drive positive organizational culture through communication is by promoting effective public speaking. Public speaking goes beyond delivering speeches to large audiences; it encompasses any form of communication where you are addressing a group of people. It could be a team meeting, a presentation, or even a casual conversation during a lunch break.

The benefits of public speaking are numerous. Firstly, it helps to build confidence. By regularly speaking in front of others, you become more comfortable expressing your thoughts and ideas, leading to increased self-assurance in all areas of your work. Secondly, public speaking enhances your ability to articulate your message clearly and concisely. This skill is invaluable when it comes to conveying complex information, persuading others, and inspiring action.

Furthermore, public speaking enhances your leadership skills. As a leader, your ability to communicate effectively can significantly influence the culture of your organization. By delivering compelling speeches, you can motivate and inspire your team, fostering a positive and high-performing work environment.

For employees, developing public speaking skills can help them become effective advocates for their ideas and contribute to the growth of the organization. It allows individuals to share their knowledge and expertise, leading to increased collaboration and innovation across teams.

In conclusion, communication plays a vital role in driving positive organizational culture. By promoting effective public speaking, individuals at all levels can enhance their communication skills, foster collaboration, and create a positive work environment. Developing these skills benefits not only the individual but also the organization as a whole. Therefore, it is essential for everyone to recognize the importance of communication and actively work towards improving their communication abilities.

Enabling Collaboration and Teamwork

In today's fast-paced and interconnected world, collaboration and teamwork have become essential skills for success in any field. The ability to work effectively with others, share ideas, and jointly solve problems is crucial in achieving common goals and driving innovation. In this subchapter, we will explore the significance of enabling collaboration and teamwork, and how effective communication through public speaking can greatly contribute to these endeavors.

Collaboration and teamwork offer numerous benefits, both at the individual and organizational level. By bringing together diverse perspectives, skills, and experiences, teams can tap into a wider range of ideas and knowledge. This diversity fosters creativity and innovation, leading to better problem-solving and decision-making. Furthermore, collaboration enhances employee engagement and satisfaction, as individuals feel valued and included in the decision-making process. It also promotes a sense of belonging and camaraderie, creating a positive work environment.

Public speaking plays a vital role in enabling collaboration and teamwork. Effective communication skills are the cornerstone of successful collaboration, as they enable individuals to express their thoughts, ideas, and concerns clearly and persuasively. Whether it's presenting a project proposal, sharing updates, or facilitating brainstorming sessions, public speaking allows individuals to articulate their vision and inspire others to join their cause. By mastering the art of public speaking, individuals can communicate their ideas with confidence, engage their audience, and foster a collaborative spirit.

Another important aspect of public speaking in enabling collaboration is active listening. Effective collaboration requires individuals to actively listen to others, understand their perspectives, and build upon their ideas. Public speaking skills help individuals become better listeners by teaching them to pay attention, ask relevant questions, and respond empathetically. By actively listening, individuals can create an environment where everyone's voices are heard and respected, leading to more inclusive and effective collaboration.

Moreover, public speaking provides a platform for individuals to share their expertise and knowledge with others. By delivering informative and engaging presentations, individuals can contribute to the collective learning and growth of the team. This knowledge-sharing culture not only enhances collaboration but also builds trust and strengthens relationships within the team.

In conclusion, enabling collaboration and teamwork is crucial for success in any endeavor. Public speaking plays a pivotal role in facilitating effective communication, active listening, and knowledge sharing within teams. By mastering public speaking skills, individuals can harness the power of words to inspire, engage, and enable collaboration among team members. Whether you're a leader, employee, or student, developing your public speaking skills will undoubtedly benefit your personal and professional growth, and contribute to the overall success of your team and organization.

Achieving Success and Results through Effective Communication

In today's fast-paced world, effective communication has become more crucial than ever. Whether you are a student, a professional, an entrepreneur, or a homemaker, the ability to communicate effectively is key to achieving success and desired results in every aspect of life. This subchapter explores the benefits of public speaking and how it can enhance your communication skills, boost your confidence, and propel you towards success.

Public speaking is a powerful tool that can transform your life. It offers numerous benefits that go far beyond simply conveying information to an audience. By mastering the art of public speaking, you can develop your leadership skills, build strong relationships, and influence others in a positive way.

One of the key benefits of public speaking is the improvement it brings to your overall communication skills. When you stand in front of an audience and deliver a speech, you learn to articulate your thoughts clearly, organize your ideas effectively, and present them in a compelling manner. These skills are not only valuable in public speaking but also have a significant impact on your everyday communication, whether it is in a professional setting or personal interactions.

Additionally, public speaking boosts your self-confidence. The ability to confidently express your thoughts and ideas in front of a group of people instills a sense of self-assurance that spills over into other areas of your life. When you are confident in your communication abilities, you are more likely to take on challenges, seize opportunities, and achieve your goals.

Furthermore, public speaking provides a platform for you to share your expertise and ideas with others. By sharing your knowledge, you can inspire and motivate your audience, leading to personal and professional growth. Whether you are delivering a TED talk, presenting a business proposal, or giving a speech at a community event, your words have the power to create a lasting impact and bring about positive change.

In conclusion, effective communication is the key to success, and public speaking is a powerful tool that can help you achieve your goals. By mastering the art of public speaking, you can enhance your communication skills, boost your confidence, and influence others in a meaningful way. So, embrace the power of words, develop your public speaking skills, and unlock your full potential to achieve success and desired results in every area of life.

Conclusion: Embracing the Power of Words for Leadership Communication in Every Aspect of Life

In this book, "The Power of Words: Leadership Communication for Everyone," we have explored the tremendous benefits of public speaking and how it can positively impact your personal and professional life. Throughout the chapters, we have delved into various aspects of leadership communication and discussed strategies to enhance your skills in this area. Now, as we conclude our journey together, let us reflect on the transformative power of words and how embracing it can benefit every aspect of your life.

Communication is the cornerstone of effective leadership. Whether you are leading a team, engaging in public speaking, or simply conversing with others, the ability to articulate your thoughts clearly and persuasively is paramount. The benefits of public speaking extend far beyond the stage or boardroom; they permeate every aspect of our lives.

First and foremost, mastering the art of public speaking instills confidence. As you practice and refine your speaking skills, you will become more comfortable and self-assured in expressing your thoughts and ideas. This newfound confidence will have a ripple effect, positively impacting your personal relationships, professional endeavors, and even your own self-perception.

Furthermore, effective communication fosters stronger relationships. When you can effectively express yourself, you create a deeper connection with those around you. By mastering the power of words, you can inspire, motivate, and influence others to rally behind your vision. This is especially crucial in leadership roles, where the ability to communicate effectively is essential for driving change and achieving success.

Additionally, public speaking enhances your critical thinking and problem-solving abilities. As you engage with different perspectives and present your ideas in a coherent manner, you develop a sharper intellect and a more strategic mindset. These skills are invaluable not only in your professional life but also in personal decision-making and navigating complex situations.

Finally, embracing the power of words enables us to become more empathetic and understanding individuals. Through effective communication, we learn to listen actively, genuinely comprehend others' viewpoints, and respond with empathy. This empathy creates a harmonious environment, fostering healthier relationships and a more inclusive society.

In conclusion, the benefits of public speaking extend far beyond the stage or boardroom. By embracing the power of words and honing our leadership communication skills, we can unlock our full potential in every aspect of life. Whether it is in our personal relationships, professional endeavors, or societal interactions, effective communication is the key to success. So, let us embrace this power and embark on a journey of self-improvement and growth, knowing that our words have the potential to transform lives and create a better world for everyone.

Milton Keynes UK
Ingram Content Group UK Ltd.
UKHW020930231123
433129UK00016B/843